Ancient Hymns

FOR

CHILDREN.

LONDON:
JAMES BURNS, 17 PORTMAN STREET,
PORTMAN SQUARE.

MDCCCXLII.

In the interest of creating a more extensive selection of rare historical book reprints, we have chosen to reproduce this title even though it may possibly have occasional imperfections such as missing and blurred pages, missing text, poor pictures, markings, dark backgrounds and other reproduction issues beyond our control. Because this work is culturally important, we have made it available as a part of our commitment to protecting, preserving and promoting the world's literature. Thank you for your understanding.

Preface.

THE Hymns in this little book have been taken from the "Hymns translated from the Parisian Breviary, by the Author of the Cathedral." The object which has been kept in view in the selection has been that of adopting such only as appeared the most easy and suitable for children. A few words have been occasionally altered for that purpose.

I. W.

BISLEY,
Festival of St. Luke the Evangelist.

ANCIENT HYMNS FOR CHILDREN.

Morning.

My voice shalt Thou hear betimes, O Lord: early in the morning will I direct my prayer unto Thee, and will look up.—Psalm v. 3.

Morning lifts her dewy veil,
   With new-born blessings crown'd;
Let us haste her light to hail
   In courts of holy ground.

Christ hath shed a fairer morn,
   From darkness rising free;
In His glorious light new-born
   Let us lift the jubilee.

MORNING.

From the swaddling bands of night
    When sprang the world so fair,
Putting on her robes of light,
    O what a power was there!

When our God, who gave His Son
    His guilty foes to spare,
Woke to life the guiltless One,
    O what a love was there!

When from th' Eternal's hand
    The earth in beauty stood,
Deck'd in light at His command,
    He saw and call'd it good.

Yet a goodlier world it stood
    In the Creator's sight,
In the Lamb's all-cleansing blood
    Wash'd to celestial white.

MORNING.

In the light of rising morn,
    Which o'er creation flies,
We descry, by fancy borne,
    Heaven's courts beyond the skies.

In the image of th' Eternal—
    In Christ, of souls the sun—
Dimly, through the fleshly veil,
    We see the Holy One.

In Thy law, bless'd Trinity—
    A torch-light sure and true—
What Thou forbiddest may we flee,
    What Thou dost bid, pursue.

Noon.

The heavens declare the glory of God; and the firmament sheweth His handy work.—Psalm xix. 1.

O Thou who in the light dost dwell,
To mortal unapproachable,
Where angels veil them from Thy rays,
   And tremble as they gaze;
While us the deeps of darkness bar,
From Thy blest presence set afar,
Till brightness of th' eternal day
   Shall chase the gloom away.

Such day Thou hast in store with Thee,
Hid in Thy boundless Majesty—
Of which the sun, in glorious trim,
   Is but a shadow dim.

NOON.

Why lingers thus light's golden wheel,
Which shall to us that day reveal?
But we must cast this flesh aside
   Ere we with Thee abide.

But when the soul shall take her wing
Beyond where clouds their shadow fling;
To see Thee, praise Thee, love Thee still,
   The o'erflowing heart shall fill.
Great Three in One, form us, and bless,
In Thine unfailing bounteousness,
To pass unharm'd through this our night,
   And see Thine endless light.

Evening.

The Lord my God shall make my darkness to be light.
PSALM xviii. 28.

AND now the day is past and gone,
   Holy God, we bow to Thee;
Again, as nightly shades come on,
   To Thy sheltering side we flee.

For all the ills this day hath done
   Let our bitter sorrow plead;
And keep us from the wicked one
   When ourselves we cannot heed.

He darkly prowls Thy fold around
   In his watchful circuitings:
Father, this night let us be found
   'Neath the shadow of Thy wings.

O when shall that Thy day have come,
   Day ne'er sinking to the west;
That country and that holy home
   Where no foe shall break our rest?

Now to the Father and the Son
   We our feeble voice would raise,
With Holy Spirit join'd in One,
   And from age to age would praise.

The Lord's Day.

Ye are all the children of the light, and the children of the day: we are not of night, nor of darkness; therefore let us not sleep as do others.—1 Thess. v. 5, 6.

MORN of morn, and day of days,
Silent as the morning's rays,
From the sepulchre's dark prison
Christ, the light of lights, hath risen.
He commanded, and His word
Death and the dread darkness heard:
We, O shame, more deaf than they,
In the chains of slumber stay.
Nature 'neath the shadow lies;
Let the sons of light arise,
All throughout night's stillness deep
Holy harmonies to keep.

THE LORD'S DAY.

While the dead world sleeps around
Let the sacred temple sound;
Law and prophet, and blest psalm,
There shall breathe a holy calm.
Thus to hearts in slumber weak
Let the heavenly trumpet speak;
And, like streaks of early morn,
New ways mark the newly born.
Grant us this, and with us be,
Sole Fountain of all charity:
Thou who dost the Spirit give,
Bidding the dead letters live.
Equal praise to Father, Son,
And to Thee, the Holy One,
By whose quickening breath divine
Our dull spirits burn and shine.

Christ approaching.

Yet a little while, and He that shall come will come.
Heb. x. 37.

Our God approaches from the skies,
    Let us for Him prepare,
With sweet and solemn harmonies,
    And deep heart-glowing prayer.

Nor doth the everlasting Son
    Abhor the Virgin's womb;
That we from bondage may be won,
    He bears a servant's doom.

Gentle and meek He comes: arise,
    Sion, behold thy King,
And haste to meet Him, nor despise
    The peace He deigns to bring.

He shall return the Judge e'en now,
  On clouds with lightning driven,
And us, his children left below,
  In triumph bear to heaven.

Let crimes, the brood of night, depart
  From the approaching morn;
And the old Adam of the heart,
  For Christ is newly born.

Be praise, while endless ages run,
  To Father, ever blest;
To Spirit, and eternal Son
  In flesh made manifest.

Christ in the Manger.

Ye shall find the babe wrapped in swaddling-clothes, lying in a manger.—S. LUKE ii. 12.

INFANT, born the world to free,
    Look on us—
That in child-like wisdom we
Put on Thy humility.

Thou that midst the beasts did sleep,
    Helpless babe,
From dark foes that seek Thy sheep,
Sacred Shepherd, save and keep.

Thou who hast Thy Godhead laid
    All aside,
On the breast of mother-maid,
To our weakness lend Thine aid.

Thou who op'st the heavenly door—
  Virgin-born,
Three in One, whom we adore,
Praise to Thee for evermore.

S. Stephen.

Love your enemies, bless them that curse you, do good to them that hate you, and pray for them that despitefully use you.—S. MATT. v. 44.

HOLY Love towards her foes
In mysterious channels flows;
Bow'd to soothe, or steel'd to blame,
Holy love is still the same.

Pleader for himself he stood:
Now he falls, his eloquent blood
From the ground for mercy cries,
Pleading for his enemies.

God from heav'n His martyr heard,—
Heard, and bless'd his dying word:
Saul, the murderer, standing by,—
Saul was granted to that cry.

Thus he bow'd his drooping head,
Thus his joyous spirit fled :
" Jesu, Lord,"—his offering free,—
" Take the life I owe to Thee."

Death, kind angel, watching nigh,
Sweetly clos'd his tranquil eye;
Whilst the freed spirit wing'd her flight,
From beam to beam, to endless light.

Thou that dealt'st thy plenteous store
Daily to the sick and poor,
Now art come, a welcome guest,
To thy Father's table blest.

In thy bridal-crown display'd—
In the wedding-robe array'd,
Of thy purple life-blood wove,
For the slain One's feast of love.

Thou of Virgin-mother born,
In this wintry world forlorn,
   Jesu, Lord, all praise to Thee.
All glory be to Father, Son,
And Holy Spirit, Three in One,
   Unto all eternity.

S. John the Evangelist.

Now there was leaning on Jesus' bosom one of His disciples, whom Jesus loved.—S. John xiii. 23.

THOU whom before the rest
  The love of Jesus bless'd;
Thou darling of the incarnate Deity,
  Sharer of all His woes,
  Friend of His dying throes,
Eye-witness of His awful sovereignty.

  Too favour'd thou of Heaven—
  O thou, to whom 'twas given
To touch with mortal hand th' immortal Lord;
  With mortal ear and eye
  To hear and see Him nigh,
And hold high converse with th' eternal Word.

How mighty was the boon
    When oft to thee alone
Thy Lord in love His secret soul display'd!
    When on His mountain-throne
    To thee reveal'd He shone
Full God, full man, in Deity array'd!

    Thou, as on Jesus' breast
    All peaceful thou dost rest,
Drink'st of the living streams of Deity;
    Whilst on thy cleansed sense
    With silent influence
Thou closely steal'st His dread divinity.

    O cup too full, too high
    For poor mortality!
Thy raptur'd spirit fled its earthly clay.
    Say, when in calm repose
    Thy tranced eyelids close,
To what bright dreams of heav'n they waken, say.

O access dread, O bliss
Of mutual love, ere this
To every soul in every age unknown!
When such the altar-fire
That lights thy pure desire,
What countless rays it scatters from its throne!

Hence art thou ever proved
Loving, and ever loved;
Hence thy bright brow and virgin modesty;
Hence all that heavenly beam,
That angels might beseem,
Pour'd round thy head, a circling galaxy.

Hence o'er and o'er again
Thy thrice-repeated strain—
Whate'er thou say'st, " 'tis love, 'tis love requires:"
Scarce doth the struggling soul
Her ecstasy control,
But bursts her bonds, and vents her holy fires.

Glory on high to Thee,
Holy, eternal Three—
Father and Son and Holy Spirit blest!
Lo, this the stedfast law,
The stedfast faith we draw
From out Thy sacred fount, by Heaven's own
    hand express'd.

The Holy Innocents.

Suffer little children to come unto Me; for of such is the kingdom of heaven.—S. MATT. xix. 14.

LITTLE flowers of martyrdom,
  Whom the cruel sword hath torn,
  On the threshold of the morn—
  Rosebuds by the whirlwind shorn!

All regardless of their doom,
  'Neath the altar where they lay,
  With their palm and chaplets gay,
  Little simple ones, they play.

Tyrant, what avails their tomb?
  He shall 'scape the bloody blade
  Which hath many childless made—
  Infant born of mother-maid.

Thus the type of Him to come,
 Restorer of lost Israël,
 Moses 'scaped the tyrant fell,
 Guarded by the Invisible.

Jesu, born of Virgin's womb,
 Father, Spirit, One and Three,
 Sing we glory unto Thee—
 Sing we everlastingly.

Martyrs.

Be thou faithful unto death, and I will give thee a crown of life.—Rev. ii. 10.

Fear no more for the torturer's hand,
  Nor the dungeon dark that bound thee;
The choirs of heav'n about thee stand,
  Bright shining homes surround thee.

Fear no more for the clanking chain,
  Thou art free as light of heav'n;
The stripes that mark'd thy frame with pain
  For rays of thy crown are given.

Fear no more for stern cold, nor need,
  Nor for nakedness for ever;
Christ's pure light doth clothe thee and feed,
  And shall no more from thee sever.

Lo, He stands at His martyr's side,
    Death with nobler life surrounding,
And takes him with Him to abide,—
    The dread tyrant's wrath confounding.

To God on high be honour done,
    In the height all height exceeding;
To Father, Son, and Holy One,
    From Father and Son proceeding.

The Circumcision of Christ.

Our Saviour Jesus Christ gave himself for us, that he might redeem us from all iniquity.—Titus ii. 13.

O HAPPY day, when this our state
  With Jesus' blood was consecrate!
O happy day, when first the Lord began
To bare the arm which rescued ruin'd man!

Scarce born in this our solitude,
  The little Infant pours His blood,
To be the pledge of His eternal love,
E'en now the earnest of His death to prove.

Entering the world, His Father's will
  Instant He hastens to fulfil;
And is beforehand with the day of death,
Mark'd as the victim ere He yields His breath.

In very pity for our fall,
　He thus becomes the criminal ;
Made 'neath the law, He hastes its yoke to bear,
That from that yoke He may His people spare.

The law is slain by that same sword
　By which it dares to smite the Lord ;
A holier law begins, which shall prevail—
The holier law of love, which cannot fail.

Thee, of a Virgin-mother born,
　In whom is centred endless morn—
We praise Thee, bless Thee, worship and adore,
With Father, and with Spirit, evermore.

The Epiphany.

There shall come a Star out of Jacob, and a Sceptre shall rise out of Israel.—Numbers xxiv. 17.

WHAT is that which shines afar,
    Fairer than the sun at morn?
'Tis a glorious star,
    An Infant King's bright messenger:
It marks a cradle low, where God on earth is born.
    Faithful spake ye, seers of old,
        From Jacob doth a Star arise;
    The East is stirred to behold.
A little star keeps watch without—
        'Tis let down from the skies:
    But a nobler Star within
    Doth its march begin,
    Which, on their distant rout,
To Him, with gentle power, doth lead the Wise.

The toil and perils, what are they?
Faithful love knows no delay:
Kindred, and home, and country hold not them;
　　'Tis God that calls, and they obey.
　　　　Star of Bethlehem,
　　Star of Grace, that lead'st the way,
　　Let not the mists of our dark soul
Obstruct Thy heavenly light, and guiding soft
　　　　　control.
　　　Father, Light of lights, to Thee,
　　To Holy Spirit, and to Son,
　　In whom Thou to the world hast shone,
　　　　Everlasting glory be!

Christ crucified.

They shall look upon Me whom they have pierced.
Zech. xii. 10.

DRAW out, sad heart, thy melody,
And tell, with plaintive cry,
The sorrows of the Crucified,
The wounds of Him that died;
Him, who a willing victim came
To die a spotless Lamb.

By that unpitying fury kill'd,
Our ransom He fulfill'd:
We drink health from His bitter cup;
His cross doth lift us up;
His stripes for us a balm have found,—
'Tis He our wounds hath bound.

With feet and hands transfix'd in pain
He bursts our bonds in twain;
For us a healing fount He bore
At every bleeding pore:
The nails that hold Thee on the tree
Bind us to that and Thee.

Thy heart, now still'd by death's cold trance,
Hath pierc'd the barbed lance;
Op'ning a door to all below,
Whence blood and water flow:
On earth a fount of cleansing shewn,
In heav'n a glorious crown.

Grant, Saviour, that for us below
These fountains aye may flow,
The cup of healing here to prove,
The cup of bliss above:
Then we will ever sing Thy praise
Through Heav'n's eternal days.

Christ risen.

Death is swallowed up in victory. O death, where is thy sting? O grave, where is thy victory?
1 Cor. xv. 54, 55.

ANGELS come on joyous pinion
  Down the heav'n's melodious stair;
Triumphing o'er death's dominion
  Up to this our lower air,—
    Christ is rising,
    And doth burst the sepulchre.

All in vain the posted station
  Of the armed soldiery,—
All in vain the faithless nation
  Sets the seal and watches nigh;—
    Ye need not fear,
    None shall reach where He doth lie.

He Himself, from sleep awaking,
   Who now hidden lies in gloom,
Through your seals, and without breaking,
   Shall come forth and leave the tomb;
      Death cannot hold
   Him born of a Virgin's womb.

When His heart stern death was rending,
   They cried out, " Thy death-bed leave,
And from off Thy cross descending,
   We will upon Thee believe!"
      To death resign'd,
   He would suffer no reprieve.

No, He hath not thence descended,
   Or ye would for ever grieve;
But from death He hath ascended;
   Will ye not in Him believe?
      'Tis He alone
   Can your chains of death relieve.

Lord, with Thee in daily dying
  May we die, and with Thee rise;
And on earth, ourselves denying,
  Have our hearts within the skies,—
    To sing our God,
  Three in One, sole good and wise.

Christ ascending.

While they beheld, He was taken up, and a cloud received Him out of their sight.—Acts i. 9.

BLEST Saviour, now Thy work is done,
 Of death and hell the victory,
And Thou ascended to put on
 The glories of eternity.

Now borne upon a glittering cloud,
 Thou seest afar earth's little bound;
While, following, flock a happy crowd
 Their Saviour and their King around.

'Mid wondering angels without end
 Th' eternal doors are open wide;
While Man and God Thou dost ascend,
 To sit Thee at Thy Father's side.

Our one High-Priest, our Advocate,
   Our Intercessor there on high,
Offering for us, without the gate,
   The blood of boundless charity.

The Church Thy bride Thou dost adorn,
   And cherish her in her unrest;
And she, when harass'd and forlorn,
   Reclines upon Thy faithful breast.

Thou midst her conflicts art at hand,
   Thou o'er her head dost hold Thy shield;
By Thee alone she is sustain'd,
   By Thee hath power her arms to wield.

Where Thou our Head art gone before,
   Do Thou to Thee the body draw—
On ways where Thine own steps of yore
   Have trod Thine own life-giving law.

Now to the Father let us sing,
   And, Holy Spirit, unto Thee ;
And to our heav'n-ascended King,
   Who captive led captivity.

Christ ascended.

In my Father's house are many mansions. I go to prepare a place for you.—S. JOHN xiv. 2.

THOU, who dost build for us on high
A house beyond the crystal sky,
    Lead us to Thee above
    With cords of love.

Thou, in whom dwelleth every good,
Thyself shalt be the soul's abode,
    Waking from life's brief night
    To endless light.

Then shall we see Thee as Thou art,
Thy countenance pure, nor fear to part,
    To love Thee and adore
    For evermore.

If Thou dost love us, leave us not;
But send down from that pure calm spot,
    Pledge of adopting love,
    That fostering Dove.

Thou who shalt come our Judge to be,
Jesu, the glory be to Thee,
    With God and Spirit pure,
    Aye to endure.

Whit-Sunday.

Suddenly there came a sound from heaven, as of a rushing mighty wind; and it filled all the house where they were sitting.—Acts ii. 2.

Now our prayers are heard on high;
  And 'mid mortal men unblest,
The good Comforter is nigh,
  Coming from the Father's breast.

What mysterious sight and sound
  Of our God the coming speaks?
Like a rushing wind profound,
  All the house His presence shakes.

Like a fiery shower it falls
  All the hallow'd guests among;
Upon each within the walls
  Sitting like a flaming tongue.

While the bright and gentle blaze
  Harmless plays their heads around,
It hath gone, with piercing rays,
  To their deepest hearts' profound.

All aghast the nations throng,
  While with other tongues they name
Things that unto Heav'n belong;
  And whate'er they speak is flame.

Lo, again, O sight of fear!
  For the hearer hath a tongue;
Of new prophets, while they hear,
  Hath another harvest sprung.

Praise to Father, and to Son,
  And to Thee, the Holy One,
By whose awful breath divine
  Our dull spirits burn and shine.

To the Holy Spirit.

The Comforter, which is the Holy Ghost, whom the Father will send in my name, He shall teach you all things.
S. JOHN xiv. 26.

COME, Thou creating Spirit blest,
    And be our guest ;
And fill the hearts which Thou hast made
    With Thy sweet aid.
Thou who art call'd the Paraclete,
    From Thy blest seat,
The living fount of light and love,
    Come from above.
Thou that in sevenfold power dost stand
    At God's right hand,
And layest on the untutor'd tongue
    The Spirit's song,
Unto our senses light impart,
    Love to our heart ;

And may our flesh's infirmity
    Be strong in Thee :
May the foe's assaultings cease,
    And grant Thy peace,
That, treading in Thy footsteps blest,
    We may find rest.
May we by Thee the Father know,
    And Son below;
And Thee, the Spirit, come from both,
    Trust, nothing loath.
To Father, Son, and Holy One,
    Praise aye be done;
From whose sweet effluence divine
    We too may shine.

Christ leaving His Apostles.

In the world ye shall have tribulation: but be of good cheer; I have overcome the world.—S. John xvi. 33.

Now the hour is drawing near
   Which your Master shall remove;
Little children, do not fear,
   He shall not forego His love;
With the banner'd cross unfurl'd,
Fear no tumults of the world.

When He wills, the parting storm
   Shall a bright blue sky disclose;
Thence shall stoop joy's deathless form
   Smiling on your vanish'd foes;
While the world's brief pleasures flow
To the sea of endless woe.

He who as a brother died,
  And in the cold grave below
Laid Him by His brethren's side,
  He shall hence before you go,
And take you with Him to dwell
In Godhead unapproachable.

May we here, Lord, die with Thee,
  And with Thy true wisdom wise
Put on immortality,
  Having treasure in the skies,
Where all things with one accord
Sing the Triune holy Lord.

Lazarus rising.

He that was dead came forth, bound hand and foot with grave-clothes.—S. John xi. 44.

OPEN is the rocky tomb,
And a voice is in the gloom;
And a sound is on the ear;
And the dead that sound doth hear:
For God Himself is near.
Amazing sight! the spirit now
Hath his former seat, I trow;
For the dead doth stretch his hands
Like a babe in swaddling bands,
Darkly groping for his way
In the light of living day.
Now forth he stands
    With a stare,
Survivor of himself, and heir.

His bands about him broken lie,
Vanquish'd Death away doth fly,
Glad to resign his victory.
O Lord, this earnest of Thy sway
Gives prelude of the judgment-day.
    Thee, we pray,
When we shall resign our breath,
Save us from the second death;
From the second death us save.
So may we, rising from the wintry grave,
Through everlasting spring,
The Father, Son, and Spirit, sing.
               Amen.

Martha and Mary visited by Christ.

Martha, Martha, thou art careful and troubled about many things; but one thing is needful; and Mary hath chosen that good part.—S. LUKE x. 41, 42.

As Jesus sought His wandering sheep,
   With weary toil opprest,
He came to Martha's lowly roof
   A lov'd and honour'd guest.

Blessed art thou whose threshold poor
   Those holy feet have trod;
To wait on so divine a guest,
   And to receive thy God.

While Martha serves with busy feet,
   In reverential mood
Meek Mary sits beside the Judge,
   And feeds on heavenly food.

Yea, Martha soon herself shall sit
  The eternal Word to hear,
And shall forget the festal board,
  To feast on holier cheer.

Sole rest of all who come to Thee,
  O'er all our works preside,
That we may have in Thee at last
  The part that shall abide.

Saints Departed.

<small>God shall wipe away all tears from their eyes.—Rev. xxi. 4.</small>

Soldiers, who to Christ belong,
In your glorious faith be strong;
For God's promise it is sure;
His rewards they shall endure.

   Come away,
Where no shadows in a glass,
Where no things that come and pass
   To decay;
But the leaf that shall not fade,
And the lights that know no shade
   Ever stay.

Where the happy skies above
Are the house of them that love
   All the day;

And good spirits o'er our head,
As on happy stars they tread,
   Sing alway.

Here on earth we can but clasp
Things that perish in the grasp.
   While ye may,
Lift your faces to the skies,
God Himself shall be your prize :
   Come away.

Where the happy heavenly host
Sing Father, Son, and Holy Ghost ;
For His promise it is sure ;
His rewards they shall endure.

Faith in God.

O God, Thou art my God; early will I seek Thee.
Ps. lxiii. 1.

Thy promise, Lord, is our sure stay,
  Thy faith immoveable;
To Thee we turn at dawning day,
  To Thee our wants we tell.

Man's promise in the hour of need
  Frail as himself is found,
Which fails, and like the broken reed
  The leaning hand doth wound.

Blessed is he who in Thy breast
  Himself doth wholly hide;
No whirlwind's power shall break their rest
  Who in that Rock abide.

Lest our hearts fail, Thy hand shall hold
   With sacramental ties;
Hope, on the mighty pledge made bold,
   To endless good doth rise—

Springs to Thy throne on mercy's gleam,
   And casts aside her care;
And drinks of the celestial stream,
   Which flows for ever there.

Of grace, adored Trinity,
   The everlasting spring,
Sole hope of safety, unto Thee
   With our whole heart we cling.

Hope.

Hope thou in the Lord, and keep His way.—Ps. xxxvii. 35.

Thou dost, Lord, abhor the proud;
To the arrogant and loud
Thou hast ne'er the praise allow'd
    Which is Thine alone.

Thankless souls that will not pray,
Turn Thy gracious stream away,
And like wither'd grass decay
    'Neath the scorching noon.

As the servant's earnest gaze
Keeps his master's hand and ways,
So our eyes we ever raise
    To Thy Sion's throne.

And shouldst Thou the gift withhold,
When to Thee the heart is told,
Hope shall on her anchor hold,
    And await the boon.

Glory be to God on high,
To the Son who came to die,
To the Spirit ever nigh,
    Sealing us His own.

Communion of Saints.

By one Spirit we are all baptised into one body.
1 Cor. xii. 13.

How sweet it is to see
Brethren in unity;
The body, through whose veins
Christ's lowly Spirit reigns,
Which lives and moves in Him alone!

How sweet one voice to raise,
All in one house of praise,
Besieging heav'n's high tower
With prayer's assailing power—
Sweet force, whereby e'en God is won!

Be it from **Thee** above
That holy **house** to love;
Be peace for **ever** there,
And nothing **e'er** draw near
That shall disturb **that** union.

The God of peace, our Father's care,
  Such bonds must form and keep,
That we our brethren's joys may share,
  And weep with them that weep :
Then may His praises never cease,
Who builds us in His house of peace.

Communion of Saints.

By one Spirit we are all baptised into one body.
1 Cor. xii. 13.

How sweet it is to see
Brethren in unity;
The body, through whose veins
Christ's lowly Spirit reigns,
Which lives and moves in Him alone!

How sweet one voice to raise,
All in one house of praise,
Besieging heav'n's high tower
With prayer's assailing power—
Sweet force, whereby e'en God is won!

Be it from Thee above
That holy house to love;
Be peace for ever there,
And nothing e'er draw near
That shall disturb that union.

Woe unto such! but they
Who love Thee and obey
Shall find earth's trials rude
Turn to their endless good;
While foes but aid and help them on.

Far worse is flattery's tongue,
In soft persuasion strong,
Which, with its pleasing wiles,
Its willing prey beguiles,
And makes the thoughtless heart its own.

Grant us, blest Trinity,
The love which flows from Thee,
That we on this our road
May bear each other's load,
And reign together round Thy throne.

The Grace of God.

<small>I can do all things through Christ that strengtheneth me.
PHIL. iv. 13.</small>

MAKER of all things, aid our hands,
  In all works be near,
That our chaste lives may worthier prove
  The name of Christ to bear.

Thou, only mighty, only good,
  Art to Thyself the way;
Thou only, who hast given the law,
  Canst give us to obey.

Dangers encompass all the road:
  Our slippery feet control;
That so our steps more steadfastly
  May press on to the goal.

O happy goal, where true repose
    And peace awaits for ever;
And Thou to Thine dost give to drink
    Of joy, as from a river!

For Thee, good Lord, the heart doth pant,
    For Thee the spirit sighs;
Grant unto those Thy grace hath sav'd
    To win the eternal prize.

The Sabbath of Heaven.

Let us labour, therefore, to enter into that rest.—Heb. iv. 11.

Thou, Lord, in endless rest
 Dost Thy sure Sabbath keep,
Where angels ever blest
 Do sing and never sleep:
To us, from virtue fallen, toils belong,
For how can exiles sad sing their lost country's
 song?

But Thou wilt us restore,
 If unto Christ we flee;
Grant us to mourn still more and more
 What keeps us back from Thee;
That faith and hope may lighten earthly woes,
Until we be restored to Thy secure repose.

Thee, Lord, where in Thy rest
   Thou dost Thy Sabbath keep,
May angels ever blest
   Sing Thee, and never sleep:
Sing Father, Son, and Holy Spirit divine,
And we, though exiles sad, our feeble strain combine.

The heavenly Jerusalem.

The city had no need of the sun, neither of the moon, to shine in it: for the glory of God did lighten it, and the Lamb is the light thereof.—Rev. xxi. 23.

O HEAVENLY Jerusalem,
   Of everlasting halls,
Thrice blessed are the people
   Thou storest in thy walls!

Thou art the golden mansion,
   Where saints for ever sing;
The seat of God's own chosen,
   The palace of the King.

There God for ever sitteth,
   Himself of all the crown;
The Lamb the light that shineth,
   And never goeth down.

Nought to this seat approacheth
  Their sweet peace to molest;
They sing their God for ever,
  Nor day nor night they rest.

Calm Hope from thence is leaning—
  To her our longings bend;
No short-lived toil shall daunt us
  For joys that cannot end.

To Christ, the Sun that lightens
  His Church, above, below;
To Father, and to Spirit,
  All things created bow.

The Day of Judgment.

I saw the dead, small and great, stand before God; and the books were opened.—Rev. xx. 12.

Day of wrath!—that awful day
Shall the banner'd Cross display,
Earth in ashes melt away!

The trembling, the agony,
When His coming shall be nigh,
Who shall all things judge and try;

When the trumpet's thrilling tone,
Through the tombs of ages gone,
Summons all before the throne!

Death and Time shall stand aghast,
And Creation, at the blast,
Rise to answer for the past.

Then the volume shall be spread,
And the writing shall be read
Which shall judge the quick and dead.

Then the Judge shall sit! oh, then
All that's hid shall be made plain,
Unrequited nought remain.

What shall wretched I then plead?
Who for me shall intercede,
When the righteous scarce is freed?

King of dreadful Majesty,
Saving souls in mercy free,
Fount of Pity, save Thou me!

Bear me, Lord, in heart I pray,
Object of Thy saving way,
Lest Thou lose me on that day.

THE DAY OF JUDGMENT.

Weary seeking me wast Thou,
And for me in death didst bow;
Be Thy toils availing now!

Judge of Justice, Thee, I pray,
Grant me pardon while I may,
Ere that awful reckoning-day.

O'er my crimes I guilty groan,
Blush to think what I have done—
Spare Thy suppliant, Holy One.

Thou didst set the adultress free,
Heard'st the thief upon the tree—
Hope vouchsafing e'en to me.

Nought of Thee my prayers can claim,
Save in Thy free mercy's name:
Save me from the deathless flame!

With Thy sheep my place assign,
Separate from th' accursed line,
Set me on Thy right with Thine.

When the lost, to silence driven,
To devouring flames are given,
Call me with the blest to heaven!

Suppliant, fallen, low I bend,
My bruised heart to ashes rend;
Care Thou, Lord, for my last end!

Full of tears that day shall prove
When, from ashes rising, move

To the judgment guilty men.
Spare, Thou God of mercy, then!

Lord all-pitying, Jesu blest!
Grant them Thine eternal rest.
Amen.